Also by Marianne Brems

Sliver of Change
Unsung Offerings

In Its Own Time

poems by

Marianne Brems

Finishing Line Press
Georgetown, Kentucky

In Its Own Time

ACKNOWLEDGMENTS

"Stranger" published in *WayWords Literary Journal* August 20, 2021
"Tangles of Loss" published in *Mosaic Art & Literature Journal* June 10, 2022
"Not Too Often" published in *The Bluebird Word* February 28, 2022
"No Tug of War" published in *Vita Brevis Press* Oct. 21, 2020
"False Fruition" published in *Sledgehammer Lit* April 4, 2021
"Trust" published in *Academy of the Heart and Mind* Jan. 2019
"The Skin of Thought" published in *The Pangolin Review* June 16, 2021
"One Fresh Start" published in *Bluepepper* Oct. 10, 2020
"Something Found" published in *Trestle Ties* July 1, 2020
"Sparkle" published in *Prospectus* Winter/Spring 2022
"A Promise Broken" published in *The Fault Zone Reverse* December 12, 2021
"A Simple Stillness" published in *Remington Review* July 20, 2022

Publisher: Leah Huete de Maines
Editor: Christen Kincaid
Cover Art: Sofiia Balitckaia
Author Photo: Joan Bresnan
Cover Design: Elizabeth Maines McCleavy

Order online: www.finishinglinepress.com
also available on amazon.com

Author inquiries and mail orders:
Finishing Line Press
PO Box 1626
Georgetown, Kentucky 40324
USA

Table of Contents

Every event occurs at a time when necessary factors align.

For my sister Karen

In Its Own Time

I leave behind the pulse of the street
where appointments demand punctuality,
deadlines dictate deliveries,
traffic sets the pace,
lunch is on the clock.

I enter the heartbeat of the ICU
where my sister lies
with an infinity of blood
spilled in her brain.
Urgency is
blood pressure,
Doppler numbers,
eye movement,
all the focus of drips
from a bag of clear liquid on a pole
and recorded in the scurrying lights
of an EKG.

I stand by,
grasp for a structure
that thrives out in the street.
I sink, my head barely above water,
into an ocean of consciousness
that blood will drain
with its own distress,
with its own result,
in its own time.

Stranger

A stranger passing casts a shadow before me,
an insignificant event,
flowing like water under a bridge,
easily unnoticed as obligations dominate,
but alters us both irreversibly
as our eyes from separate tunnels
meet in a nod of acknowledgement,
a momentary validation
in the strangeness of strangers
like first rain after a drought.

Toddler

He stands outside the Walgreen's exit past the wall of pain killers.
Cardboard around his neck reads *Hungry Homeless God Bless*.
I busy myself folding my shopping list into perfect quarters.
I flatten the strip of metal in my mask snug against my nose.
Fabric clings to my mouth as I breathe in.

Back of my hand pushes a panel to open the door.
The man says *Anything you can spare is much appreciated*.
I know better, but uncertainty tightens inside me.
No matter what I give, it's not enough.
Illegal to ask for money in public?

The laughing face of a toddler in a grocery cart draws me in.
She waves at the man.
Doesn't know homeless from neighbor.
He smiles.
Her mother steers the cart a little farther away.

My feet unsettled,
digging at the pavement as I walk away,
my focus on the store window across the street.
I know I have small bills in my wallet.
We share nothing more than the warmth of afternoon sun.

Next time I want to be a toddler.

Tangles of Loss

She gets rid of crumbs,
brings in the mail,
moves the hose around the yard.
These are not things that fold
under the insistence of grief.
They merely proceed
to punctuate time and matter.

I imagine wrinkles of angst
seeping from her fingertips
as I watch her feed the dog.
Then her hand quickly smooths
the top of his head.

Married forty-one years,
his unexpected end so sudden.
It may be that lifting large boxes
while packing up the house
pushes back against
tangles of her loss.

I must remember not to open with,
How are you?
each time I greet her.

Not Too Often

It's an ordinary day,
nothing to celebrate.
She puts on
just the right hat,
at just the right angle,
not for warmth
or to protect from sun,
one to blend perfectly
with the afternoon light
in a room
where heads might turn,
not too quickly,
not all at once.
No scarf over her shoulder,
no pearls around her neck,
just a hat,
not too new,
not too old,
a style seen occasionally,
but not too often.

No Tug of War

A Golden Retriever
sits with legs splayed at random,
right front paw folded under,
as though he just fell that way
while trying to please,
really what matters most,
shoulders in a soft hunch,
gaze welcoming passersby.

He's always there
by the entrance to the pool,
a book with bears and giraffes ,
or balloons and honeysuckles
placed with care before him.

No tug of war or ball to retrieve
just quiet composure,
as if to say,
Not my world,
but I can wait a while
among these gentle strangers,
his owner counting laps
until their worlds can join
in a game of fetch,
two native speakers
of the same language.

False Fruition

False fruition or
the theory of infinitely expandable time.
It's the familiar rule of restlessness.
The more the minutes close in,
the more time casts an ever wider net.
Just hang the socks or check the mail
and infant moments are born.
Calculate the seconds,
halve the time,
and you'll just make it,
or not,
before a door shuts.

Transformation

My brain eliminates the need for tulips
to sprout inside my skull,
no mud, no mess, or weeds to pull,
just invisible pixels
casting a succulent garden before me,
even in darkness.

An image brilliant on its own,
but filled with possibilities—
Which best complements tulips—
daffodils or iris?
Which the ideal month to plant—
October or November?
Which the optimum shape for beds—
square or irregular?

When words emerge
to set this image in flight,
as if their exact order,
their sound,
the number of syllables,
their kernel,
had no greater purpose;
they transform
cotyledon to leaf,
bud to blossom,
red to crimson.

Cabinet of Options

The door to the cabinet of options
is open just a crack
to let out one or more possible solutions
to a lock refusing to catch
or a boy who won't eat broccoli.

The sliding closet door
may include in its darkness
a treasure or two lost for years.
Best to leave a sliver of light
should such gems come forward.

Or in a drawer
next to the socks
but beneath the trousers
might lie one or more answers
to the Riddle of the Sphinx,
undiscovered
if not for some tiny open space.

Closure can be tempting
to make things nice and neat,
but consider the cost
of shutting off avenues
where possibilities may hibernate.

Change

Yesterday's gentle *good morning*
is to today's intrusion on quiet.

The hole where I once cinched my belt
is now one further over.

The straight legs of jeans
turned flared, then back again.

A mind set to refuse help
unsets as someone listens.

A toddler pushes up vertical
to take nascent steps.

A window shade closes
a little earlier each afternoon.

Rocks become rounded.

Elastic sags.

Skin shrivels.

Milk curdles.

Paint dries.

And when someone dies
nothing is ever the same.

Change, no beginning, no end,
shapes lives
without diffidence or concern.

Trust

Within the quiet interstices
in our conversations,
small voiceless moments of trust
in sheep's clothing
bring our humanity together
like nickels to magnets.

Trust that our message
can sustain suspension.

Trust that this suspension
can enhance our message.

Trust that we can stand tall
in our tolerance for silence.

Trust that we can wait
after saying *I hate to tell you, but...*

Discomfort may tug at our eyes,
but should we turn away,
we always turn back again.

The Skin of Thought

A word is not a crystal, transparent and unchanging; it is the
skin of living thought and changes from day to day as does the
air around us.
    —Oliver Wendell Holmes, Jr.

Scattered and unruly,
thoughts slither in at all hours.
We then specify and contain
their inexactness in a skin of words.

Like the flesh we live in,
that secures
blood, bone, organs,
and expands during
reach, retraction, intake,
these words,
contract and relax,
bend and billow,
as they wrap around fluid thought.

They pass through us
like the air we breathe,
gathering new meanings as they go;
they a plural plus a singular pronoun,
mask so much more than a face covering.

One Fresh Start

I spill wine that darkens my carpet.
I know this scar,
like jaws around my throat
will remind me daily of my carelessness.

I attack the stain with sparkling water
and vigorous rubbing.
To my surprise, all traces vanish,
handing me one fresh start
in a broken world.

I return for a moment to a time

before I learned my mother
couldn't fix the pain
of skinned knees,

before I knew that pieces
fall into place only after many
have not,

before I found skin color
more of a constant
than the growth of tree rings,

before I saw a world
where hate doesn't disappear,
it just hides under rocks
until someone comes along
and kicks them away.

Something Found

When something lost turns up,
a circle completes
like rebirth
that spreads soft colors
into the moment.

Equilibrium surfaces
like health after illness.
Muscles regain plasticity.
Steps lighten.

Assets restored.
A balance retaken
on a road less congested.

Bridges

Like a parent, bridges lead us by the hand
over obstacles impassible without them,
a feat unmatched by houses or buildings.

Each bridge comes to fruition
with little ambiguity
at a point of common need.

When we cross their requisite spans,
a simple equalization occurs.
No one passes above another.

All have equal capacity
to travel from one side to the other.
All meet the same desired end.

Bridges harbor no judgment,
belong to everyone,
connect through necessity's open arms.

Yard Sale

In a driveway, on a tarp
lie forks and spoons in mixed patterns
essential for big meals when kids came home,
mismatched wine glasses some chipped,
a bowl from a long ago visit to the Notre Dame,
a sky blue vase with gold trimmed leaves.
All have sat on a shelf behind something heavy
for a duration no one remembers.

Then, within the march of practical pursuits,
a yard sale comes to life.
Value springs back as an empty space,
an extra dollar,
the chance to gratify another's yen
for flawless blue,
value as pleasing as any new purchase,
but lasts only as long as fresh eyes
see splendor in one-time treasures.

Sparkle

My maple cabinets fresh with a woody fragrance,
my glossy new floor without scuffs or scrapes,
my gleaming quarter-turn faucets
all put a leap in the step of my kitchen,
a lightness in my sternum
as I stand in the midst of rebirth.

As I stay longer,
I hear ghosts of this well-worn nest
burping in the woodwork,
a cabinet attached millimeters from a wall,
a floorboard unequal in height to another,
the refrigerator leaning half a centimeter to the left.

This ever maturing house—
fraying in places
with the echoes of roots below
and walls that swell and constrict
as conversations turn to
broken hearts, grandchildren, cancer—
still sparkles in a new set of clothes.

Leaves in the Sun

Edges of brown
crisp to the touch,
withered and wanting,
under the pale azure sky
of an early autumn day.

Spinning and Churning

I turn my spinning and churning
over to clouds
that collide and reshape above me.
A bearded face looks down,
cheeks pushing over eyes
as a billowy mass rises,
dissipating features
into loose wisps of hair.

A tiny jet,
scrappy and quick,
leaves a crisp white tail
that soon softens,
then vanishes entirely
into consummate blue.

Urgencies inside me loosen
as I float dreamlike
within these evolving vapors,
free for minutes
from colorless obligations
in a crowded earthly meadow.

A Promise Broken

Air should sit by for a time
in a comfortable chair
or pass with only a flutter of movement.
It should walk softly in loose clothing
bearing sunlight or quenching rain.

It was not meant to be seen,
nor to be thick or viscous,
or leave particles in lungs and eyes.
It was not meant to lock out
the light of high noon.

But as host
to a tyrant of our own making,
the ground shifts,
the rules change,
and a promise is broken.

A promise
that shakes me by the shoulder
as days of acrid smoky haze
thrust their weight upon the landscape
and make me want to cry *Uncle*.

A Season Halted

The grass on route to dark green
as rain fades.
Stalks hunger for fullness of color.
Soon spent, they grow
little beyond a nappy carpet
of pale green and beige
barely covering hard bloodless earth
usually fertile, soft, forgiving
at this time of year.

Clouds intermittently cluster,
shades of gray
shuffling with promise,
compounding against one another
but refusing to release rain.

Blades shrivel,
roots condense,
each folding inward,
for an untimely hibernation,
the season for
spreading,
reaching,
expanding skyward
halted without anchor,
swallowed whole.

A Simple Stillness

A Great Blue Heron scans a river bed
with deep elegant wingbeats,
then folds her wings for landing.
Her long sinewy toes spread lightly
on marsh grass.
She stands motionless as in a photograph,
focused,
assured,
patient
as time slows before prey swims near.

No clicks.
No likes.
No busy screens
or noise inside her head.

Amidst the urgency of sustenance,
just a simple story of stillness
like the last line in a book
before the cover closes.

Marianne Brems has an MA in Creative Writing from San Francisco State University. She is a long time writer of nonfiction and her publications include textbooks in her teaching area of English as a Second Language and several trade books. She began writing poetry in mid-life to capture essence and order in random events of daily life. She has a special interest in writing poems that exhibit a strong sense of the natural world. She is the author of the chapbooks *Sliver of Change* (Finishing Line Press 2020) and *Unsung Offerings* (Finishing Line Press 2021). Her poems have also appeared in several literary journals including *The Bluebird Word, Front Porch Review, Remington Review, Green Ink Poetry,* and *Scarlet Leaf Review.* She lives, cycles, and swims in Northern California. Website: www.mariannebrems.com.

www.ingramcontent.com/pod-product-compliance
Lightning Source LLC
Chambersburg PA
CBHW030052100426
42734CB00038B/1493